ISBN 978-1-332-83541-6
PIBN 10166200

1 MONTH OF
FREE
READING

at
www.ForgottenBooks.com

By purchasing this book you are eligible for one month membership to ForgottenBooks.com, giving you unlimited access to our entire collection of over 1,000,000 titles via our web site and mobile apps.

To claim your free month visit:
www.forgottenbooks.com/free166200

English
Français
Deutsche
Italiano
Español
Português

www.forgottenbooks.com

Mythology Photography **Fiction**
Fishing Christianity **Art** Cooking
Essays Buddhism Freemasonry
Medicine **Biology** Music **Ancient
Egypt** Evolution Carpentry Physics
Dance Geology **Mathematics** Fitness
Shakespeare **Folklore** Yoga Marketing
Confidence Immortality Biographies
Poetry **Psychology** Witchcraft
Electronics Chemistry History **Law**
Accounting **Philosophy** Anthropology
Alchemy Drama Quantum Mechanics
Atheism Sexual Health **Ancient History**
Entrepreneurship Languages Sport
Paleontology Needlework Islam
Metaphysics Investment Archaeology
Parenting Statistics Criminology
Motivational

The Anti-Trust Laws
ith Special Reference to the Mennen Co. Decisio
The Hardwood Lumber Decision
And the Edge Resolution

An Address by

FELIX H. LEVY
Of the New York Bar
Former Special Counsel to Dept. of Justice

Delivered Before the

AMERICAN SUPPLY & MACHINERY
MANUFACTURERS ASSOCIATION

At Its Annual Convention

Held at

ATLANTIC CITY, N. J.

May 9, 1922.

THE ANTI-TRUST LAWS, WITH SPECIAL REFERENCE TO THE MENNEN CO. DECISION, THE HARDWOOD LUMBER DECISION, AND THE EDGE RESOLUTION.

Mr. Chairman and members of the Convention: I desire at the outset to express my appreciation and thanks for the privilege involved in your invitation to appear before you to-day. Upon the courteous suggestion of your Secretary, Mr. Mitchell, I came here from New York a day or two in advance of the time set for my address. The result has been that I have been able to mingle with you and to listen yesterday, with more than ordinary interest, to the proceedings of your Convention so that, if I may say so, I feel in a certain sense like one of your number rather than like a stranger from without the gates.

I also had the opportunity of reading the stenographer's transcript of the proceedings of your recent Birmingham Convention, and I hope you will believe that I say it not in idle words of flattery but with sincerity and as an observer outside of your own field of combat, who perhaps therefore can get a better perspective, that I have rarely read anything of more genuine interest than the proceedings of that Convention.

I listened yesterday with great interest not merely to the general proceedings of your Convention, but also to the eloquent and inspiring address by Captain Gorby on "optimism". And then, when I reflected on the proceedings of your Birmingham Convention and, without making invidious comparisons, bore in mind the masterly presentation of various topics affecting not merely your own industry but also the country at large, by your President, Mr. Gladding, and the scholarly and statesmanlike speech made by Mr. Williams, I felt like adding to the catalogue pronounced by Captain Gorby of the elements and items which ought to make us all optimistic, the further element that a country which possesses an industry like yours, containing men of the marked talents and vision shown by Mr. Gladding and Mr. Williams and by many others of your membership, that a country possessing such men need not fear for its future.

If the majority of the members of the two houses of Congress, were customarily men of the business experience and acumen and of the vision and foresight of men like Mr. Gladding and Mr. Williams, the welfare of our country would be greatly promoted.

The gentlemen whom I have thus named, leaders in your industry, are but types of the forceful, aggressive and far-sighted men who are to be found in every kind of industrial activity in this country. Are our business men—endowed as they are with rare gifts of energy, initiative and vision—free to use their talents without hindrance? They are not, for, as I shall endeavor to demonstrate to you today, they are shackled and fettered by antiquated and out-worn legal doctrines which have long ago been abandoned by Great Britain and by all other civilized countries. I refer to the ancient common-law doctrine known as "restraint of trade", a doctrine born in England centuries ago to meet conditions then existing but now utterly changed.

In England, with a system of jurisprudence vastly superior to our own, the changed conditions of modern business have progressively brought about an amelioration of this ancient legal principle, so that today it rests very lightly upon the shoulders of British industry; whereas in this country it retains, virtually without change, its old-time rigor, to the great detriment, as I shall endeavor to show, of our trade and commerce.

Economists who have studied the subject, maintain that the greatest obstacle and hindrance to the legitimate exercise of their natural powers and capabilities by the business men of our country, is to be found in our own laws, framed by our own servants, interpreted and enforced by our own officials. For such is the situation which the Anti-Trust Laws of the United States have created as a result of a grave and fundamental misconception which has befallen those laws.

I shall devote a brief part of your time to a discussion of the history and the evolution of the Sherman Law.

It was passed in 1890 for a definite, distinct and exact purpose. It was passed in order to disrupt, and prevent the

4

recurrence of, great trusts—the whiskey trust, the oil trust, the sugar trust, and the like. The debates in Congress indisputably show that to be the only purpose for which the Sherman Law was enacted. To a substantial extent it has performed that duty. In breaking up, ineffectually, the oil trust and the tobacco trust, the Sherman Law was not at fault, but the officials were at fault who permitted farcical dissolutions of those trusts—dissolutions which resulted in the greater enrichment of the owners of those monopolies, but in little or no benefit to the public. But that is not a criticism of the Sherman Law. Court decisions without number show, on the contrary, that it has performed, in a very substantial degree, the purpose for which that law was enacted.

But when we examine the subject further, what do we find? We find that the operation of that law has been extended far beyond its original purpose of breaking up these great combinations which did so much harm. They did great harm, indeed. They did things which were oppressive and wicked and, as Mr. Chief Justice Taft once said, it would "make you choke" to think that men would do to others what the conductors of those great trusts did to their small rivals. The result was that the people of this country were so inflamed, their righteous indignation was so aroused, that it has not yet cooled off and they have permitted that law to be extended to the multitudinous details of daily business, so that there is scarcely an act that a merchant or a manufacturer can do by way of concert with his competitor, which is lawful. As everyone knows, it prohibits the discussion of price agreements. You would be just as indictable for making a price agreement, or an agreement to prevent overlapping of territory, as if, by way of illustration, you committed arson. It is a crime in the one instance and in the other.

A speaker who preceded me at your Convention, said that this is "the most governed and the worst governed country on earth". I adopt his phrase as a basis for saying that there is not a country on earth that has a law which is interpreted as is our Sherman Law. I took the trouble before I came here to look up the laws of England on this subject. Now, I think England is a pretty good example with respect to industrial matters. Napoleon called it a nation of shop-keepers and Britain is proud of the appellation. I believe the controlling thought of Lloyd George at Genoa today is the restoration of trade activity, because that is the mainspring of the life of nations.

The decisions of the English Courts are plainly to the effect that cooperative activities of business competitors, which are declared unlawful by our Sherman Law, are entirely lawful in England. Striking confirmation of this fact is furnished by the definition or description of trade associations given in the "Encyclopaedia Brittanica", as showing the functions of such associations in England. It is stated in these words:— "Those which are themselves engaged in trade, ... or which result from the combination of firms or individuals in the same or connected trades, for the purpose of facilitating or restricting production, limiting competition, regulating prices, etc.". This is an open, avowed public declaration that such is the purpose of trade associations in Great Britain. What a striking contrast it presents to the permissible activities of trade associations in this country! And now to show you that in England the purposes thus stated are in fact performed, I shall read to you briefly from a notable book, treating of trade practices in Great Britain. It is written by a learned professor, Prof. Macrosty of the University of Birmingham, and is entitled "The Trust Movement in British Industry". The book shows that every industry in Great Britain has a trade association. The author, in describing their functions and purposes, says: "Price Associations, the next highest grade, aim at the regulation of sale prices as well as of the conditions of bargaining, and exhibit a great variety of structure. . . . . The simplest form is where the manufacturers or traders meet, either as individuals or as members of an association for general trade purposes and determine on a rise in prices to meet some special circumstance, such as an increase in the price of raw materials. The agreed rise may either be for an indefinite period so long as the conditions remain the same, or for a fixed period, after which competition is once more free. Thus we find the Associations of Coal Masters raising the price of coal at the beginning of Winter and Associations of Grocers trying to make the retail price of sugar follow advances in the wholesale price. The next stage is where the members combine for a definite period, usually a year, for the specific purpose of fixing prices from time to time."

6

It goes without saying that procedure of this nature on the part of trade associations in this country would be grossly violative of the Sherman Law. In order, however, to show you that this procedure in England is done openly and not under cover, and is done without legal interference, I call your attention to these succeeding statements made by Prof. Macrosty, in which he specifically names two associations. In succeeding sentences of his book other associations are also named, but time will not permit me to read them now.

His further statement to which I refer, is this: "Regulation may take place irregularly as trade demands, as is done by the Fife Coal Association, or normally at meetings weekly, monthly, or even quarterly, as in the case of the Midland Unmarked Bar Association. . . . . Generally speaking, the rules of a Price Association provide the ordinary machinery of a Committee, President, Secretary and Treasurer, annual and other meetings. Sometimes a deposit of money, or securities, or a promissory note is required, out of which penalties for breach of the rules are levied." (Laughter).

When you consider the contrast which the foregoing statement of conditions prevailing in England present, as compared with the conditions affecting trade associations in this country, you may well laugh. Of course, in speaking thus, I do not mean to be flippant, for the subject involves too many serious aspects to be treated jestingly. I venture to suggest, as I shall later more fully point out, that if Secretary Hoover, in his laudable efforts to increase the efficiency of trade associations in this country, would investigate the conditions thus shown as prevailing in England, and determine whether the more liberal policy prevailing in England may not, at least to some extent, be utilized in this country, he would greatly advance the useful efforts which he has been making in behalf of trade association activities.

It may be said by the advocate of the strict enforcement of the Sherman Law, that the practices thus disclosed as prevailing in England are done without sanction of law. I have, however, shown that they are done publicly and openly, and I will now show that they have the highest judicial sanction and support. I refer to the important decision rendered in 1912 by the Privy Council of England, one of the highest courts in that country, in a case which has become widely known as the Australian Collieries case.

That important case arose in the following manner. The great and progressive commonwealth of Australia has a statute largely resembling our Sherman Law; but, as you will see, very differently enforced. Some years ago the entire coal industry of Australia got together in one combination; the members of the combination were the coal operators, the coal-carrying steamships and railways, the wholesalers and the retailers. Now that is A to Z, from the ground to the consumer. They got together and agreed on how much each operator should produce, at what price he should sell, what freight rates the railroads and steamships should charge, and at what price the retailer should buy and should sell. And a suit was brought by the Attorney-General of the Commonwealth of Australia, who asserted that this was a violation of the law; but the Privy Council declared it lawful and stated:

"It can, in their Lordships' opinion, never be of real benefit to the consumers of coal that colliery proprietors should carry on their business at a loss, or that any profit they make should depend on the miner's wages being reduced to a minimum. Where these conditions prevail, the less remunerative collieries will be closed down, there will be great loss of capital, miners will be thrown out of employment, less coal will be produced and prices will consequently rise until it becomes possible to re-open the closed collieries or open other seams. The consumers of coal will lose in the long run if the colliery proprietors do not make fair profits or the miners do not receive fair wages."

Now, I say, that is an astonishing statement when contrasted with Court decisions in like cases in this country, and with the speeches you hear in Congress. For there they say that the only one to be considered is the ultimate consumer, that anything that prevents prices being reduced is detrimental to the public, that therefore competition must be carried on to the ,uttermost extreme and that competitors cannot get together in great emergencies and say, "We agree that the price should be raised thus and so", in order that weaker members of an industry shall not be ruined. The prevailing American argument is that competition is the life of trade. The distinguished Judge who wrote the sentence which I have read to you, apparently believed that if competition is the life of trade, it is usually the death of the competitors.

It is not open to the slightest question that if a situation similar to that which was disclosed in the Australian Collieries case had been presented to the courts of this country under the Sherman Law, our courts would have declared the combination thus disclosed to be unlawful. Indeed, there is not the slightest doubt that persons comprising such combination would, under the Sherman Law, have been subject to indictment and criminal prosecution.

It will be observed that the controlling thought in the minds of the Privy Council, which led it to declare the Australian Collieries agreement to be lawful, was that such agreement enabled the parties thereto to conduct their business without loss, and that consumers of coal would "lose in the long run if the colliery proprietors do not make fair profits". In other words, the principle upon which the decision was based is that competitors should be permitted to combine if such a course is necessary in order to prevent the closing down of the less remunerative units in the industry, and the consequent loss of capital and reduction of the number of men employed in the industry.

The courts of this country, in their decisions under the Sherman Law, have acted in direct disregard and contradiction of this principle. This is amply shown in numerous decisions of our Supreme Court, of which the following are typical instances. In the famous Danbury Hatters' case, the Supreme Court declared certain acts to be unlawful, although, to use the Court's words, "the impelling motive of the combination was an effort to better the conditions of the combiners, which, except for the anti-trust act, might be proper and lawful". In another decision, the Supreme Court used the following language:

> "It is argued that the main purpose of this agreement being to increase the trade of the parties, to enhance competition in a larger field, and improve the character of the product, these objects are beneficial to the public as well as to the private parties, lawful

in their scope and purpose, and justifying the indirect and partial restraint of trade involved in the execution of the agreement . . . . Wider markets and more trade may be the inducements to such agreements, but they are purposes which the Act of Congress does not permit to interfere with the freedom of interstate traffic."

In another case, the Supreme Court, speaking of the provisions of the Sherman Law, said:

"Nor can they be evaded by good motives. The law has its own measure of right and wrong, of what it permits or forbids, and the judgment of the courts cannot be set up against it in a supposed accommodation, of its policy with the good intention of the parties, and it may be, of some good results."

The comprehensive contradiction involved in the words just quoted, to the principle upon which the Privy Council acted in the Collieries case, is strikingly obvious. Our Supreme Court viewed the case then before it from Alpha to Omega, that is, from its motives or inception, to its results or conclusion; and stated that even though its inception be characterized by good motives, and its conclusion be characterized by good results, the provisions of the Sherman Law may nevertheless declare it to be unlawful. Can sharper contrast between the liberal policy of England and the drastic policy of our country on this important subject be conceived? Can any man, properly informed, doubt the severity, not to say the harshness, of our Sherman Law?

It is hard to realize that such contradictory conditions can exist in Great Britain and in the United States. The principle which I have shown as prevailing in England, prevails in all other countries except ours. We are the only country on earth which forbids cooperation. Why, the very principle of our Government is, in a way, symbolized by the motto "e pluribus unum", out of many, one, meaning strength from union, or by the other motto, "united we stand, divided we fall." Children's copy books are full of these maxims. But our laws say you cannot cooperate. You cannot cooperate on anything that is really vital to your business progress, such as

10

prices, territory, production and the like. Why, during the
depth of the business crisis last year, in my practice, which
often consists of advising trade associations and groups of
manufacturers, a number of them came to me in an unnamed
industry—I mean one I must leave unnamed—and said, "We
are in a terrible condition; we were prosperous in the flush
period which has just passed, but now we are nearly 'broke' and
if we continue to operate our factories we will be 'broke'; there
are about fifty belonging to our group and we find it a most
urgent business necessity to shut down our factories". And
they said to me, "Can we under the Sherman Law through our
trade association pass a resolution that our factories shall be
closed up?" And,I said, "If you do, you will violate the law.
It involves a curtailment of your unrestricted competition and
it is unlawful." And they said, "We are not going 'broke' by
virtue of any such notion as that; and we will shut our factories. We absolve you from any blame. We will shut our
factories." They shut the factories and thereby husbanded and
retrenched their resources and when times improved they
opened them again and were ready to go on and continue business, but they violated the law in doing it as surely as if they
had violated the law against grand larceny, burglary or any
other like offense.

This is a very extraordinary situation. It is very extraordinary that manufacturers and merchants should be forbidden from cooperating with one another in matters like those
which I have mentioned, where such cooperation would be
clearly beneficial to them and to their industry. But the laws
of this country forbid such cooperation. In my opinion that
is a very extraordinary situation. The reason for it is that
the public in this country has regarded with suspicion all
acts of cooperation among competitors, ever since the flagrant
violations practised by the great and notorious trusts in the
earlier days—violations which the Sherman Law was enacted
to prevent and for the continued prevention of which that law
should be maintained. Still affected and influenced by the
righteous wrath of a time that has gone, Congress has set its
face implacably against any amelioration of that law, which,
in this country alone, of all countries on earth, compels its able
and farsighted leaders of industry to refrain from utilizing one
of the most important and fundamental factors in the promo-

11

tion of efficiency, namely, cooperation, and forces them to cut one another's throats in relentless competition.

But, I beg that in what I have said and shall say today, I will not be misunderstood as seeking to justify the many instances of wrongful restraints of trade which still exist in this country, or as advocating the repeal, or even the relaxation in severity, of the statutes which are intended to prevent and to punish monopolistic practices and injurious agreements calculated to hinder free competition with resultant detriment to the public and to the commonwealth. I hope you will pardon the personal element when I say that I regard with pride the fact that for a period of some years under President Roosevelt's administration, I was of Government Counsel in the prosecution of one of the great trusts, so that it is but natural that I should regard with approval, as indeed I do, the power given to the Government by the Sherman Law to disrupt the great monopolistic aggregations of capital which, until a decade ago. infested the highways of commerce in this country. It is often said in Congress and elsewhere that the Sherman Law has proven ineffectual, or, as it was called on the floor of the Senate a few days ago, a "dead-letter". The basis for this characterization is believed by expert students of the subject to be the ineffective decrees of dissolution in the Standard Oil case and the Tobacco Trust case. That these decrees were ineffective in the restoration of true competitive conditions, and particularly in the creation of a new situation whereby independent competition on the part of relatively small traders could arise and flourish, cannot be doubted. But those who have carefully studied the subject agree that it is equally indisputable that the unfortunate outcome of the Government's prosecution of those two notorious trusts under the Sherman Law, was in no way attributable to any defect or weakness in that Statute, but was due entirely to the way in which the decrees of the Supreme Court directing the disintegration of those great monopolies, were executed. Authorities agree that the Sherman Law, as an agency and an instrument for the disruption and repressing of trusts or other like monopolistic combinations, is the embodiment of the highest legislative and judicial wisdom. It was the creation of the most able lawyers who have been members of the United States Senate since the Civil War.

Even the most hostile critic of the effectiveness of the

Sherman Law will not question its potency and infinite value when he recalls that that Law was the basis upon which the Government rested its prosecution of the Northern Securities Company—a prosecution which resulted in complete success, namely, a decree of the Supreme Court directing the dismemberment of the Securities Company and the release of the two great railway systems which had been held in its grasp. History will record many achievements of that great American, Theodore Roosevelt, upon which his imperishable fame will be founded; but it is a matter of regret to students of economics that it will not be long remembered that it was Theodore Roosevelt, as President of the United States, who directed the prosecution of the Northern Securities Co. and pressed it to a successful conclusion. His brave and far-sighted action in so doing ought, indeed, to be inscribed high up on the roll of the courageous and patriotic deeds performed by him to the lasting benefit of his countrymen, for it is generally admitted that if he had not thus successfully invoked the power of the law against the Northern Securities Co., all of the railway systems of the land would speedily have been brought within the grasp and control of a small number of "holding" corporations similar to the Northern Securities Company, these "holding" companies, in turn, controlled by a small group of men, with a resultant condition which would have been truly menacing to the well-being of the Republic.

There is high authority for the statement which I have just made to the effect that the Sherman Law, in bringing about the disruption of the Northern Securities Co., proved its inestimable value to this country. In an address recently delivered by Mr. Justice Clarke, an Associate Justice of the Supreme Court of the United States, he said, referring to the Northern Securities case, that if the Supreme Court had decided that case against the Government, and had thereby decreed the legality of the Northern Securities Co.,

"no man can overstate what the effect would have been upon our country. If the case had been decided the other way and men had been left free, through corporate organization, to combine the other great transportation lines of the country and other great departments of business, it seems very clear that our free institutions would long ere this have been subjected to a test of strength and endurance to which every patriot must hope they may never be exposed. This one case · . . . illustrates the fact that the scope of the jurisdiction of the Supreme Court has become so fateful that the effects of many of its decisions upon the welfare of our country are as great as would be the results of decisive battles in a great war."

I submit that the forceful language just quoted, emanating from the high source from which it did emanate, is proof of the highest character that the Sherman Law has proven of immeasurable value to our country, and that it ought forever to remain upon our statute books as a warning and as a deterent to great monopolistic aggregations of capital which, until their power was broken by the force of the Sherman Law, threatened, as has been so aptly expressed by Mr. Justice Clarke, the very existence of the Republic.

I hold no brief for "big business" in the sense that I would seek to mitigate or condone the wrongful and oppressive methods which, a decade or more ago, were frequently used by the great corporations of this country. We all remember the public indignation that was aroused by the methods employed years ago by the oil trust, the whiskey trust, the sugar trust, the tobacco trust and other like monopolies. We also well remember the irregular practices of the railway companies with respect to the granting of secret rebates. I challenge, however, contradiction by any student of the subject who is well versed therein, of the statement that these practices have to a substantially complete extent been abandoned. Such abandonment, it will also, I think, be agreed, was the result of the exertion, primarily under the leadership of President Roosevelt, of the majesty of the law as embodied in the Sherman Act, and in the statutes forbidding rebating. In these respects, the Sherman Law has fully vindicated its wisdom. It follows that the criticisms of that statute so often heard in Congress and on the political hustings, to the effect that it is a "dead-letter" or that it has been "emasculated" (both of these expressions are much favored by critics of the Sherman Law), have no basis in fact.

Many other instances, quite familiar to the expert student

14

of the subject, could be cited where the Supreme Court, acting under the Sherman Law, has issued decrees of drastic and compelling force in bringing about the disruption of other great combinations.

No man, versed in the subject, can, therefore, doubt the high wisdom and effectiveness of the Sherman Law in its disruptive force and power against the great trusts; and no right-minded and patriotic man, so versed, could wish that the force and power of the Sherman Law, in that respect, should be abated one "jot or tittle". In what has just been said, I am by no means unmindful of the decision of the Supreme Court which declared the U. S. Steel Corporation (the so-called "Steel Trust") to be lawful under the Sherman Law. An adequate exposition of the distinction thus involved would require more time than is permissible on this occasion. The steel industry is so closely related to your own, that I venture to believe that such an exposition would be interesting to you and I indulge the hope that at some later Convention of your Association, I may be given the privilege of presenting the legal aspects of the "Steel Trust" decision, as showing that the Sherman Law still remains as the most drastic and efficient statute of that character upon the statute-books of any country on earth.

Nor, in what I have said and shall say today, am I unmindful of the shocking disclosures recently made and still being made in New York City by the Lockwood Committee under the guidance of that brilliant lawyer and cross-examiner, Samuel Untermyer. With a display of skill and of incredible industry amounting to genius, he has uncovered and disclosed a congeries of unlawful combinations and practices, both on the part of capital and of labor, that has astonished and shocked the country. No man in his senses, would dream of condoning such offenses, nor dare to suggest any amelioration of the laws which proscribe such grave misdeeds.

But even Mr. Untermyer, with a sense of discrimination which justly denotes, and does credit to, his high abilities, admits, I believe, that there are many forms of co-operative activity among competitors, now forbidden by law, which could with advantage to all, be made lawful, provided that the exercise of such co-operative power be placed under suitable governmental supervision so that it may not be abused. In that, if

15

I may say so, I fully concur. In short, my contention is only that the statutory condemnation against co-operative agreements should be based upon a common-sense foundation of just discrimination, to the end that on the one hand oppressive and injurious combinations or agreements in restraint of trade should as now be deemed unlawful, while on the other hand, co-operative agreements among competitors, calculated to promote, and resulting in the promotion of, the general welfare of an industry and of the general public, should, under adequate supervision, be deemed lawful and permissible. By so doing, this country would but take its place by the side of Great Britain—good company, I make bold to say, in the high enterprise of commercial and industrial progress.

I find that I have trespassed upon your time and patience so much that I must, with all dispatch, proceed to some particular phases of the subject having a special application to your industry, and other like industries.

There have recently been two further developments of the law of this subject intimately affecting the trade and commerce of this country. One is the recent decision of the Federal Trade Comission in the Mennen Co. case, and the other is the decision of the United States Supreme Court in what is known as the Hardwood Lumber Co. case. I read in the report of your proceedings at your recent convention held last month at Birmingham, Ala., that a letter was read by your president from some business concern calling attention to the Mennen Co. decision and asking the attitude of your Association concerning it; and that it was referred to this adjourned meeting of your convention now being held at Atlantic City. So, with your permission, I shall say something about the Mennen decision.

THE MENNEN CO. DECISION

By way of appreciation of your courteous invitation to address you here today, and in order that I might be able to discuss that decision more intelligently, I have obtained from the Federal Trade Commission at Washington, all of the papers and documents necessary to an understanding of the decision in that case. As a result of a close study of these papers, I feel justified in asserting that it is a most surprising decision.

16

In substance the Mennen case is this: Complaint was made against the Mennen Co. to the effect that they would not give the same discount and therefore would not make the same prices for the same quantities, to non-wholesalers as they would to wholesalers. Apparently, in that industry there had been developed a system of cooperative buying, by which retailers grouped themselves together and bought through a common source in what may be called wholesale quantities, and the Mennen Co. refused to give to the retailers thus purchasing in wholesale quantities the same price as it gave to wholesalers. Apparently, the position taken by the Mennen Co. was that the wholesalers were a necessary part of the plan of distribution of that company, being in substance, you might say, salesmen of the company, so that it seemed to the company to be good policy and calculated to advance the best interests of the company to give a lower price to wholesalers than to retailers even where the latter purchased the same quantities as the former. The subject was fully considered by the Federal Trade Commission which reached the astonishing conclusion that this procedure on the part of the Mennen Co. is unlawful.

With all of the respect and deference that a law-abiding citizen must have for a governmental tribunal, I venture to assert that this decision is wrong and cannot prevail. I have here the brief of the Government counsel showing that he based his demand that the Commission decide against the Mennen Co., upon the contention that the company's procedure violated Section 2 of the Clayton Law. There never was a greater misconception as to a proposition of law, as I respectfully believe. Section 2 of the Clayton Law says in substance:

"It shall be unlawful for any person engaged in commerce . . . . either directly or indirectly to discriminate in price between different purchasers of commodities . . . . where the effect of such discrimination may be to substantially lessen competition or tend to create a monopoly in any line of commerce."

Basing his contention upon the mere letter of this section as thus quoted, and, as I respectfully believe, disregarding its

17

history and its true intent as disclosed by such history, and overlooking court decisions to the contrary, the Government counsel claimed in his brief, and the Federal Trade Commission sustained the claim, that the Mennen Co. violated that section. In my opinion, it did no such thing. Any one who has studied the history of the Clayton Law knows that Section 2 was enacted for a totally different purpose. The section was written in order to prevent the recurrence of practices frequently employed by the great trusts in former years. For example, the records of the Federal courts will show that some years ago there was a minor cigarette company in the South which had begun to make a cigarette which proved attractive and a good seller, so that this minor company was beginning to make some headway in the cigarette industry. Thereupon the Tobacco Trust, in order to choke off and destroy the competition of this minor company, started to sell a certain very popular cigarette in the same territory in which the minor company was selling its product, and, in order to prevent the latter company from having a market for its product, the Tobacco Trust not only cut the selling price of its popular cigarette in that territory but actually gave away packets of its cigarettes gratis on the streets of towns in the territory in which the minor company was selling its product. During this time the Trust was selling its popular cigarette throughout the rest of the country at its regular prices. The result of the discrimination thus practiced by it against the minor company was only what might have been expected. Confronted with the vast power of the Trust and unable to meet the ruinous competition mentioned, the minor company failed in business and went into bankruptcy. The court records will show similar discriminatory methods which, in days now long past, the Standard Oil Trust employed to drive out of existence smaller competitors in particular territories. The purpose and the effect of such procedure is manifest. The two trusts just mentioned, and, perhaps, other trusts, resorted to a species of discrimination in prices for the avowed purpose of driving out of existence particular competitors in particular districts or territories. It is this character of discrimination against which Section 2 of the Clayton Law is aimed. In substance, that section says to manufacturers occupying a dominating position in an industry:

"You cannot go into a particular district where some competitor is selling his product in competition with your product, and by discriminating in the sales price of your product in that territory as compared with your regular selling price elsewhere, drive that competitor out of existence. For, experience has shown that, with the power you possess, you can keep up this price-cutting procedure until you drive your competitor out of existence and then you will restore your prices in that district to the same level as you have maintained throughout the rest of the country, the final result being that the community in question has been deprived of the existence of a business establishment whose continued existence would be helpful to the community, and you have caused loss to the owners of the competing industry which you have thus destroyed and have driven into bankruptcy. This procedure shall not be permitted, and, accordingly, this section forbids you 'to discriminate in price between different purchasers of commodities', that is, between the purchasers of your commodities in the particular district referred to as compared with the purchasers of your commodities in the rest of the country, for the result of such discrimination will be 'to substantially lessen competition or tend to create a monopoly' in your line of business."

The point which I am now endeavoring to present is of the essence of the matter under consideration, and I therefore desire to emphasize that, in my opinion, the true intent and meaning of Section 2 of the Clayton Law was to prevent concerns of the nature of the great trusts which occupy a dominating position in their respective industries from destroying *competitors* by discriminating in prices the territory in which such competitors operate, while maintaining their regular prices elsewhere.

But the situation occupied by the Mennen Co. is quite different. It is not claimed by the Government, nor can it be claimed, that the procedure adopted by that Company has hurt or can hurt any *competitor* of that Company. The Mennen Co., by the procedure referred to, does not aim, nor could it, if it wished to, aim ·to drive out of business some competitor or

19

some particular brand manufactured by a competitor. The effect and purpose of the Mennen system is to encourage and keep alive wholesalers as a necessary element in the company's scheme of distribution. This could not be done if retailers, grouping themselves together and thereby being able to purchase in wholesale quantities, should be able to obtain from the Mennen Co. the same price as the wholesaler obtains. Obviously in such a case the wholesaler would lose the business which he would otherwise obtain from the retailer, for if the latter were unable to obtain the wholesaler's price from Mennen Co., he would make his purchases from the wholesaler. If the requirement of the decision made by the Federal Trade Commission should be carried to its logical conclusion, it would mean the destruction of the wholesaler. Clearly this would be to the great disadvantage of Mennen Co. and of other like large manufacturers. For with the multiplicity of articles dealt in by such manufacturers, with the infinitely varied quantities which retailers from time to time require, with the vast number of accounts which the manufacturer would have to carry, clearly the cost of doing business on the part of the manufacturer would be enormously increased if he were deprived of the wholesale scheme of distribution and were compelled to make his sales directly to the retailer. I digress to say that every merchant knows that there are some lines of industry where the number of articles dealt in are not numerous and the quantities required by retailers are not necessarily small and the number of accounts dealt in not necessarily large, where direct dealing by the manufacturer with the retailer is economically possible. But in a business like Mennen's, and, for example, in the dry goods business, the jewelry business, the hardware business, and the like, it is not economically feasible for the manufacturer to deal directly with the retailer. I repeat that it is presumably upon this sound economic basis that Mennen has established his policy of preferential treatment of wholesalers. The Federal Trade Commission has, however, in this important decision, declared this to be unlawful and in violation of the Clayton Law.

I have stated that, in my opinion, the decision is contrary to the purpose for which Section 2 of the Clayton Law was enacted. I now venture to go a step further and to say that this decision is directly in conflict with two of the most recent decisions of the United States Supreme Court under the Sherman Law, namely, its decision in the Colgate & Co. case and in the Beech-Nut Packing Co. case. In those cases Colgate & Co. and the Beech-Nut Co., respectively, undertook to require their customers to observe certain resale prices by refusing to sell such customers as failed to observe such prices. In both of those cases, the Supreme Court decided that this was lawful. I may add that the Federal Trade Commission, in the Beech-Nut Co. case, had declared it unlawful and was reversed by the Supreme Court in that respect.

The language used by the Supreme Court on this point in the Beech-Nut case is:

"It is settled that, in prosecutions under the Sherman Act, a trader is not guilty of violating its terms who simply refuses to sell to others, and he may withhold his goods from those who will not sell them at the prices which he fixes for their resale."

Now you will observe that, although the Supreme Court said, in substance, "You are not compelled to sell your customer at all if you do not wish to do so", the Federal Trade Commission now says to the Mennen Co. "You must for like quantities sell to the retailer at the same price as you sell to the wholesaler." This is equivalent to saying to the Mennen Co. "that you are obliged to sell to the retailer and also that you are obliged to sell to him, for the same quantities, at the same price as you sell to the wholesaler." I respectfully submit that, as a matter of law, this dictum involves a contradiction of the decisions of the Supreme Court in the Colgate and in the Beech-Nut cases.

Now, permit me to read to you from the brief of the Government counsel in the Mennen case, where he sums up the accusations made against the Mennen Co. and points out what he claims to be the objects that Mennen had in mind in establishing the policy under consideration. He says the purposes of Mennen were threefold; namely, that, in making a discrimination in price as between wholesaler and non-wholesaler his purpose was, first, to force the resale of its products at its suggested prices. I submit that the Supreme Court, in the Colgate and Beech-Nut cases, has decided that Mennen had a perfect right to do this.

Second, that the object of Mennen was "to penalize efficiency and economy." I say, quite respectfully, that it seems incredible that such a proposition should be seriously asserted. But it was asserted, in the words as above quoted, by the Government counsel. I venture to say that it is a surprising thing to assert of Mennen, or of any business concern, that its object under any circumstances is "to penalize efficiency and economy." Of course, what was meant was that Mennen, in endeavoring to keep alive the wholesale scheme of distribution, was tending to minimize the field of operations sought to be occupied by what are known as "cooperative purchasing agencies". I shall not stop to explain the meaning of this term, as it is well understood by you and by merchants generally. But surely Mennen did not have in mind any onslaught upon such purchasing agencies, or any purpose to penalize them, or to lessen their efficiency. His aim clearly was to keep alive the wholesaler as a necessary element in his scheme of distribution; and if in doing so the "cooperative purchasing agencies" should lose business or otherwise suffer, clearly this was not because Mennen was endeavoring to "penalize efficiency and economy".

Can you imagine the executive head of the Mennen Co., or any sane executive head of any business concern, having in his mind or in his heart any such foolish—nay, detestable— purpose as the "penalizing of efficiency and economy"? And yet the Government counsel has seriously urged this as one of the motives actuating the Mennen Co. in the matter now under consideration.

The third purpose stated by the Government counsel is to "satisfy complaints and demands of individual members of the National Wholesale Drug Association—competitors of cooperative wholesale houses".

Now, what is there wrong about that, either legally or morally? Under what kind of a government are we living if Mennen has not the right to endeavor to please its customers, if it does so by methods which are economically, morally, and legally correct? Clearly the procedure is unobjectionable from an economic and a moral standpoint. And with all confidence I venture the assertion that no legal decision can be cited to show that such a procedure is objectionable from a *legal* standpoint, bearing in mind that the objection as above quoted which was made by the Government counsel is that Mennen sought to satisfy the complaints and demands of *individual members* of the Drug Association. There are decisions that, if a manfacturer yields to the *united* demands of the members of an association thereby acting under the coercion of numbers, it may be unlawful. But there is no decision which holds that a manufacturer may not of his own free will and accord meet the *individual* requests or demands of the members of an association. I respectfully submit that none of these three grounds of objection urged by the Government counsel and sustained by the Federal Trade Commission, is sound in law. And yet they are the accusations made against the Mennen Co. which have resulted in the Federal Trade Commission denouncing the policy established by that Company.

I respectfully, and with all deference, venture to say that the order thus made by the Commission will not stand, if, as provided by law, it is reviewed by the Circuit Court. I cannot imagine that any court of law would permit such an order to stand.

THE HARDWOOD LUMBER DECISION

The next topic which I shall discuss is the decision of the Supreme Court rendered a year or so ago in the Hardwood Lumber case. This was a prosecution instituted by the Government under the Sherman Law against a number of associations and companies in the hardwood lumber business. In the aggregate they constituted an important proportion of the hardwood lumber industry. They had formed an "open price competition system", and the evidence showed that they had pushed to the full limit, the possibilities afforded by such a system for the fixing of prices and the curtailment of production.

Advocates of the open price plan contend that the purpose of such plan is merely to acquaint its members with prices in past transactions. They argue that thereby members are placed in a more intelligent position to conduct their business, inasmuch as a knowledge of the trend of prices in past transactions will enable them the better to forecast the future tendency of prices and in that way the members will be able to govern their selling policies more judiciously. Such advocates contend, however, that the open price plan is not intended to be the basis or the medium, and is in fact not the basis or the medium, for agreeing upon or fixing future prices or for doing anything with respect to curtailing production by concerted agreement.

The court records in the Hardwood Lumber case show that the Supreme Court viewed the purposes of the open price plan employed in that case as having the definite purpose and result of fixing future prices and of curtailing production. In other words, the Supreme Court decided that the open price plan was employed in that instance not for the limited purposes urged by its advocates, namely, the obtaining of information as to past transactions, but was employed to the full limit of its possibilities for the purpose of fixing by agreement future prices, and, likewise, for the purpose of agreeing upon a curtailment of production. I quote the following from the opinion of the Supreme Court in that case:

"But not only does the record thus show a persistent purpose to encourage members to unite in pressing for higher and higher prices, without regard to cost, but there are many admissions by members, not only that this was the purpose of the 'plan' but that it was fully realized . . . . the 'plan' is, essentially, simply an expansion of the gentleman's agreement of former days, skilfully devised to evade the law. To call it open competition because the meetings were nominally open to the public . . . cannot conceal the fact that the fundamental purpose of the 'plan' was to procure 'harmonious' individual action among a large number of naturally competing dealers with respect to the volume of production and prices . . . ."

Inasmuch as the Sherman Law by its own plain language, reinforced by countless decisions of the Federal Courts, has indisputably declared to be unlawful, concerted action among competitors for the purpose of fixing prices and regulating production, nothing is more natural than that the Supreme Court should declare, as it did declare, the plan thus pursued in the Hardwood Lumber case to be unlawful. As the Sherman Law now stands, the Supreme Court could not reasonably do otherwise. It is quite another thing to argue that, from an economic standpoint, agreements with respect to prices and with respect to production, under suitable supervision and for the purpose of meeting industrial emergencies, are commendable and should be deemed lawful. In Great Britain, as has been pointed out, such is the law of the land. But it is not the law of this land, and the Supreme Court, in my opinion, decided the lumber case correctly; and I venture to predict that it will stand hereafter as a correct interpretation of the Sherman Law until and unless that law shall in that respect be amended.

THE EDGE RESOLUTION

What I have just said brings me logically to a consideration of the third topic which I desire to present to you today, namely, the brave and commendable but difficult enterprise undertaken by Senator Edge, of New Jersey, as embodied in what has now become widely known as the "Edge Resolution". The resolution is thus entitled:

> "Joint Resolution creating a committee to investigate existing conditions of industry and commerce in the United States for the purpose of recommending to Congress legislation defining the rights and limitations of cooperative organizations as distinguished from illicit combinations in restraint of trade."

The resolution was elaborately debated on the floor of the Senate, on April 17, 1922, but no action was taken thereon. These debates contain the statement made by Senator Edge that he is not a lawyer. Although the subject involves questions of a strictly legal nature, Senator Edge, with commendable courage and animated by the laudable purpose of liberating trade associations and the industries of the country generally, from the handicaps imposed by the Sherman Law, undertook to present and to argue his resolution although he knew he would be confronted, as he was in fact confronted, by astute lawyers in the Senate who look upon any amendment of the Sherman Law with horror.

The substance of Senator Edge's argument is that the decision in the Hardwood Lumber case has caused such obscurity on the part of trade associations with respect to the meaning of the Sherman Law and of its application to trade association activities, as greatly to hamper their efficiency.

I regard the effort which Senator Edge is making as most commendable, and, while I believe that he has set in motion a suggestion which will eventually accomplish much good, I am, nevertheless, strongly of the opinion that he is in error when he states to be the basis of his resolution, the correction of obscurity growing out of the Hardwood Lumber decision, and when he further states, as he did state in the Senate debates, that he did not aim at any amendment of the Sherman Law for the purpose of carrying out his object of liberating trade associations from the handicap under which they are now resting. I say that, in my opinion, he was in error in saying that there is any obscurity in the Hardwood Lumber decision, because there is, in fact, no obscurity. It is the same thing that we have heard throughout the country for years past, namely, that business men do not know what they may lawfully do or may not lawfully do under the Sherman Law. That assertion is not correct for, in the broadest sense, they do, or can, know what they may do and what they may not do, if they take the least effort to find out. Leaving aside mere matters of administration or of executive management, they cannot do anything lawfully under the Sherman Law which is in the nature of genuine and practical cooperation, such as is freely permitted in Great Britain and in all other countries except this. The Hardwood Lumber decision does not in the least involve any obscurity in this respect. It definitely and clearly declares that trade associations may not lawfully fix prices or agree upon production. The obscurity to which Senator Edge alludes is not with respect to what that decision *means;* but with respect to the *wisdom* of the law upon which the decision is based. In other words, the question should not be, "What does the Hardwood decision mean" for its meaning is plain enough, but the question should be, "Why is it the law as shown in the Hardwood decision, that trade associations are prevented from acting in cooperation with respect to those subjects which, above all others, require cooperation, namely, the fixing of prices when an emergency requires it, and the curtailment of production when an emergency requires such curtailment?" Of course this question should not com-

26

prise the consideration of such a right when an emergency does not exist, nor when the purpose is to fix prices extortionately, nor when the production is curtailed so as to do damage to the community. In such instances the law should remain as it is. But where the continued existence of an industry in the face of some emergency requires concerted and cooperative action with respect to the fixing of prices and the curtailment of production, it seems most logical and natural that such cooperation should be permitted. This is true in England and in all other civilized countries except ours. I have read to you today, but it is worth reading again, the illuminating statement made by one of the distinguished judges of the Privy Council of England in the Australian Collieries case as follows:

"It can, in their Lordship's opinion, never be of real benefit to the consumers of coal that colliery proprietors should carry on their business at a loss, or that any profit they make should depend on the miners' wages being reduced to a minimum . . . . The consumers of coal will lose in the long run if the colliery proprietors do not make fair profits or the miners do not receive fair wages."

Now I submit that when Senator Edge was confronted by objections made by other senators to the effect that any amendment of the Sherman Law was not to be dreamed of, his correct reply should have been:

"My resolution is not aimed at clearing up any obscurity in the Hardwood decision, for there is no such obscurity. It is intended to liberate the trade associations of this country and likewise the legitimate trade and commerce of this country, as distinguished from illicit combinations in restraint of trade and as distinguished from trusts and monopolies, from the antiquated and illogical handicap placed upon them by the Sherman Law in forbidding resort to cooperative agreements where the result of such agreements will be beneficial to the industries involved and not injurious to the community at large. The Commission which the Edge Resolution seeks to create should be given the power to investigate this important subject in order to ascertain why it is that, in this country

27

alone, trade associations and merchants generally are forbidden to act in concert with respect to questions like prices and production, even if such concerted action be necessary for the continued existence of an industry and cannot be harmful to the community. In other words, the Edge Resolution boldly asserts that the Sherman Law, in its just effort to repress trusts and other monopolistic combinations, has gone too far and commits a grave injury to the commercial welfare of this country by extending its prohibitions to concerted action upon the part of legitimate business units possessing no power or purpose of creating a monopoly. The Edge Resolution therefore aims at an amendment to the Sherman Law which will provide that, under suitable governmental control and supervision, trade associations and competitors generally may agree with one another as to prices, as to production, and as to other like fundamental matters, all of which are now forbidden by the Sherman Law.

"In conclusion, the Edge Resolution asserts that the obscurity which now exists is not an obscurity as to the meaning of the law, but an obscurity as to why it is that the law of this country, ignoring the dictates of sound economy, disregarding the well-considered doctrines and judicial decisions of a leading commercial country like Great Britain, forbids its merchants from acting in harmony with one another and compels them to compete with one another in the dark and to the extent of relentless, cut-throat hostility."

SECRETARY HOOVER'S EFFORTS

Now, with all possible respect and admiration for Mr. Secretary Hoover, whose notable achievements during the European War have gained for him lasting fame, I venture to point out that Mr. Hoover is laboring under the same misapprehension with respect to this important subject as Senator Edge has labored. I think it was on the same day upon which the Senate debated the Edge Resolution, namely, April 17, 1922, that Secretary Hoover met in his office in Washington, by his own invitation, from five hundred to one thousand secretaries of important trade associations for the purpose of discussing the means whereby the efficiency of such associations could be promoted. In doing this Mr. Hoover did a most commendable thing, for the trade associations of this country —and I refer to those whose purposes are entirely legitimate and proper—have been and are laboring under great disadvantages—disadvantages which I respectfully believe are unjustly and unnecessarily placed upon them by the laws of this land.

I respectfully believe that just as Senator Edge has overlooked the fact that trade associations are not handicapped by any obscurity in the law, but are handicapped by definite barriers created by the law, so, also, Mr. Hoover has overlooked the like fact.

I believe that Mr. Hoover will perform a service to his country equal in its importance to the inestimably valuable services which he has already rendered, if he will boldly state that the Sherman Law requires amendment for the reason that it forbids cooperation among merchants in broad fields where cooperation is vitally important; that no other country does this; that other countries like Great Britain have forged far ahead of us in the world's commerce; that they have done so largely because of the handicaps placed by our laws upon the trade and commerce of this country; that these laws should be amended so as to permit such cooperation in the same manner that is permitted in Great Britain; that such permission should be safeguarded against the abuses which human cupidity has shown will arise, by the creation of suitable Governmental supervision and control in order to make sure that the permission thus given will not be abused by utilizing it for the purpose of practising extortion or suppressing competition or creating monopoly.

The courts of England have found no difficulty in thus safeguarding the similar liberty given by the laws of Great Britain to the merchants of Great Britain. There can be no reason why similar safeguards cannot be established and enforced in this country, to the end that the merchants of this country (I speak of plain business units and not of great monopolistic combinations) may be liberated from the obstacles and barriers imposed upon them by the laws of this country—

obstacles and barriers which check their initiative, impair their energies, prevent reasonable and sensible cooperation and drive them, against their will and against their interests, into relentless and senseless competition with one another.

THE SUGGESTED REMEDY

I believe that if the state of the law on this subject, which has resulted in such an anomalous and potentially hurtful decision as that which was rendered in the Mennen case, and which has been exemplified in the Hardwood Lumber case, and which Senator Edge and likewise Secretary Hoover have by mistaken methods, laudably sought to correct—if this state of the law of this country were plainly set forth before the people of this country and before the Congress of this country, a just understanding of the subject would result, and a just and proper discrimination would be created with respect to the distinction between the wrongful practices of monopolistic combinations and the beneficial activities arising from cooperative measures on the part of plain merchants—all to the end that the incubus and burden placed upon the trade and commerce of this country shall be removed and our merchants placed upon a par with the merchants of Great Britain. We have all recently read the courageous statement made by Senator Borah, of Idaho, a man of statesmanlike stature and calibre. He had the courage, a few weeks ago, to say on the floor of the Senate that, even if it cost him his re-election, his conscience compelled him to declare himself in opposition to the so-called "Bonus Bill", because he thought it was based upon erroneous financial, economic and patriotic foundations. I venture to suggest that, if statesmen of the courage and foresight of Senator Edge and of Senator Borah (others also could be named), could, through the efforts of trade associations such as yours, acting in conjunction with other like important associations, be persuaded to take up this subject in the forceful and vigorous manner in which both of these distinguished senators have taken up and pressed forward other important measures, a proper understanding of the question would result and, remedial legislation would be adopted whereby the difficulties which I have mentioned as resting upon the industries of this country would be corrected and the merchants of this country be placed upon an even footing with the merchants of Great Britain and of other countries, all to the lasting benefit and advancement of the trade and commerce of the United States.

CONCLUSION

I beg your indulgence for a final word. The trade and commerce of the entire world has been shaken to its foundations by the destructive effects of the European War. The countries of Europe are, for the most part, bankrupt. The business of this country during the years 1920-1921 underwent an experience the like of which has not been seen since the Civil War. Bankruptcies occurred to an amazing extent. It is generally believed that, except for the beneficial influence of the Federal Reserve Law, the number of bankruptcies would have been vastly increased. Many business concerns which were not driven into actual bankruptcy, have to a large extent been so impaired financially that they are barely able to continue. It is generally believed that the worst of this condition has passed and that the commerce of this country is gradually regaining its vitality. While this recovery will be steadily progressive, the best opinion is that a period of years must elapse before the commerce of this country will regain its normal vigor and prosperity. This slowness of recovery will be attributable largely to the badly crippled condition of most of the European countries, especially Russia and the countries formerly known as the "Central Empires".

Under these circumstances can any reasonable man doubt that there is a paramount duty upon the part of the public of this country and upon the part of the Congress of this country, to view the problems which beset the business men of this country, with a sympathetic and a helpful mind—to the end that the business of this country may be placed in the most advantageous position to overcome the difficulties which now rest upon it as a result of the most destructive war that human history has recorded; and to the end that the business of this country may be equipped to regain its former position of vigor and prosperity and to meet the competition of the business men of other countries upon an equal footing?

Finally, if "in union there is strength", if it be admitte
that cooperation is a natural human tendency, and if it k
admitted that the laws of Great Britain have found a way b
which cooperation among its merchants is permitted withou
at the same time permitting injury to the Commonwealth, wh
may not this country throw off the burden which is the nega
tion of all of the foregoing and by suitable amendment of it
laws permit its merchants helpfully to cooperate with on
another and no longer be obliged, against their will and agains
the general interests of the Republic, to destroy óne anothe

PRESS, NEW YORI

CPSIA information can be obtained
at www.ICGtesting.com
Printed in the USA
BVHW04s0905031018

529154BV00027B/1008/P